An opinionated guide to

# LONDON
# PUBS

*Written by*
MATTHEW CURTIS

*Edited by*
HARRY ADÈS

*Photography by*
ORLANDO GILI

*Sutton Arms (no. 1)*

# INFORMATION IS DEAD.
# LONG LIVE OPINION.

London is overflowing with pubs. In fact it's overflowing with guides about pubs. Why another?

Well, this book cuts through the froth. We tell you only what you need to know and no more. Think of us as distillers. Less is more. Drink up our heady advice.

You see, if you were to come and stay in our spare room and ask us where to have a good pint these are the places we'd send you, confident you'd come back happy (not wasted), willing to spend another night and ask our advice again. Stay as long as you like.

Other opinionated guides:

| | |
|---|---|
| *East London* | *Big Kids' London* |
| *London Architecture* | *Art London* |
| *Vegan London* | *Free London* |
| *London Green Spaces* | *Queer London* |
| *Independent London* | *London Delis* |
| *London Pubs* | *London Hotels* |
| *Sweet London* | *Historic London* |
| *Kids' London* | *Margate* |
| *Escape London* | *Brighton* |
| *Eco London* | *Cycle London* |

*Prospect of Whitby (no.18)*

*The Palm Tree (no.17)*

*Mc & Sons (no.32)*

# THE JOY OF A GOOD PUB

What makes a pub special? Perhaps it's the particular allure of pub fabric – glazed tiles and hand-painted signs, etched glass and mirrors, velvet and leather, Elizabethan timber or 1930s brick and stone. Maybe it's the inherent cosiness, the space we choose to spend hours in conversation and laughter with good friends. Or the recent rise in their gastronomic appeal, and the promise of food and wine every bit as good as any restaurant. Or possibly that intangible thing, the vibe: a feeling, a sense of place, comfort and wellbeing that only the very best pubs possess.

And, of course, let's not forget the beer – the heart and soul of the pub. What lies unseen in their cellars can define the greatest drinking spots, but remains hidden from all but regulars in the know. This guide lets you in on that local knowledge.

London is home to an extravagant number of pubs, around 3,500 at last count. Sifting the true gems from the tired old boozers, the West End tourist traps and painfully pretentious hipster hangouts, can be overwhelming. We've cut through the noise to bring you London's very best pubs. Whether you're searching out Michelin-starred dining, a lively evening out, a relaxing Sunday lunch, or the finest ales known to humanity, we've found the pubs that fit the bill.

We need pubs now more than ever, just as they need us. Their importance was pulled sharply into focus in 2020, when the coronavirus pandemic forced them to close for months on end. Normally turning over upwards of £20 billion a year and employing up to half-a-million people, the British pub sector was dealt a hammer blow – at a time when many were struggling to stay open anyway. Pubs urgently need us for their survival, particularly independent free houses and small family businesses. We're proud that many of the pubs featured in this guide are independents; it's a real pleasure to include them in these pages.

In the same blow, we lost access to some of our most used and valuable social spaces, many of which served as vital hubs for local communities. More than just places to have a drink and a bite and gossip with friends, pubs are also where the big things happen: where we meet our partners' parents or our friends' new-born children for the very first time; where we hold our wedding bashes and funeral wakes; where we break up, get together, fall out and make up all over again. In fact, the humble pub provides the backdrop, soundtrack and catering for any number of our most memorable, significant and life-affirming occasions.

So don't hold back. Let's get out there as soon as we can. Let's keep meeting up and living the highlights of our lives in these special, special places.

*Matthew Curtis*
London, January 2021

# THE BEST FOR...

### Craft beers and real ales

You don't have to know the difference between craft beer and real ale to appreciate the rich flavours of an artisanal pint. The good folks at The Pembury Tavern (no.22), The Harp (no.8), The Kings Arms (no.23) and Joyce (no.24) will definitely lead you to the finest brews.

### Fine dining

The days when pub grub meant pork scratchings and a pickled egg are long gone, but the cooking at The Anchor & Hope (no.29) Marksman (no.20), The Harwood Arms (no.39) and The Duke of Richmond (no.13) is so good it puts many restaurants to shame.

### Independent free houses

Outside the clutches of the big breweries and hospitality chains, family-run pubs such as Sutton Arms (no.1) and Old Fountain (no.12), and plucky independents like The Cock Tavern (no.16), are doing it their own way with singular energy and flair.

### Sunday roasts

It's the meal the entire week's been leading up to – ideally topped off with a giant Yorkshire pudding. And gravy. Pubs live and die on the quality of their roasts, but at The Garrison (no.26), The Drapers Arms (no.48), The Bull & Last (no.51), The Flask (no.40) and The Axe (no.42), you're in safe hands.

### Live music

Whether it's jazz, as at The Southampton Arms (no.51) and The Wenlock Arms (no.41), folk at The Ivy House (no.31), Irish bands at Mc & Sons (no.32) or just a proper old knees-up at The Palm Tree (no.17), there's nothing like live music to lift your mood.

### Nightlife

When most publicans are polishing glasses and bolting the doors, the party's just getting started at The Three Johns (no.45), The White Horse (no.28) and Well and Bucket (no.15). Expect music, dancing and a slow start in the morning.

### Peace and quiet

Some rare pubs like The Champion (no.9), The Pineapple (no.50), and The Wenlock Arms (no.41) have a special quality of calm, perhaps even just at off-peak times, when you can truly have your thoughts to yourself.

### Beer gardens

The outdoor spaces at Chesham Arms (no.14), The Flask (no.40) and The Windsor Castle (no.37) may not boast landscaped grounds and peacocks, but they're all you need to enjoy the sun on your cheeks and a pint in your hand.

### Families

Contrary to popular belief, parenthood doesn't spell the end of your pub-going days. The Union Tavern (no.34), The Holly Bush (no.43) and The White Horse (no.38) all welcome families and recognise that parents are often in dire need of a pint too.

1

# SUTTON ARMS

*Family-run free house and old-style boozer*

A 'proper boozer' is quite a rare thing these days. That's why the 'ordinariness' of its patterned carpet and furniture actually tells you that the Sutton Arms is anything but ordinary. First off, it's been run by the same family, the Duignans, for decades, so there's an instant warmth and friendliness to proceedings, plus real care about what's on offer. An exceptionally well-curated list of beer and real ales goes hand in glove with spot-hitting Ogleshield cheese toasties, while sweet tooths are catered for with their colourful vegan cupcakes, courtesy of Duiggy Bakes.

*16 Great Sutton Street, EC1V 0DH*
*Nearest station: Barbican*
*suttonarms.co.uk  @suttonarms*

2

# THE LAMB

*Victorian jewel in Bloomsbury*

Lamb's Conduit Street sees top-notch shops and restaurants come and go, but pints have been gratefully sunk at The Lamb since the 1720s. The décor is only slightly more up to date, with gorgeous emerald glazed tiles clothing the exterior and original Victorian 'snob screens' around the horseshoe bar, which defended the privacy of old-time gents from prying eyes. There's nothing to be shy about here, though – seasonal British dishes and all-too-quaffable cask and craft ales are best enjoyed in one of the high-backed leather-buttoned seats.

*94 Lamb's Conduit Street, WC1N 3LZ*
*Nearest station: Russell Square*
*thelamblondon.com  @lamb.bloomsbury*

3

# JOHN SNOW

*Thronging Soho institution with bags of charm*

The scientist John Snow, after whom this pub is named, realised that beer drinkers were far less likely to get cholera than those using the local water pump – showing, among other things, that beer can be good for your health. So get stuck in! Hopefully, it's not so busy you'll have to forego the charming Victorian-style interior and stand outside by the aforementioned water pump. There's a Samuel Smith house beer for everyone, from Old Brewery Bitter drawn from an oak cask to bottled Yorkshire Stingo, a rare treat but dangerous at 9%.

*39 Broadwick Street, W1F 9QJ*
*Nearest station: Oxford Circus*

4

# THE FRENCH HOUSE

*Famed Dean Street haunt of bohemians*

Long fabled for all kinds of Soho shenanigans, this institution and enduring magnet for creatives, artists and louche wastrels continues to encapsulate what we all imagine Soho once was and should still be. The people here make the myth, but the underlying root of its appeal over the years has always been its killer wine list (ask Jeffrey Bernard), including 30 champagnes, and the brilliance of its Gallic-accented food. Vive la légende!

*49 Dean Street, W1D 5BG*
*Nearest station: Leicester Square*
*frenchhousesoho.com  @frenchhousesoho*

5

# THE JERUSALEM TAVERN

*Ancient glory with a modern twist*

Nab one of the few battered chairs and you'd never guess that this time-warp of a pub – with its beer-furrowed tables, flaking panels and windowpanes like a Dickensian apothecary – is only 30 years old, not 300. The illusion is achieved courtesy of the genuinely old building, tight corners, awkward crannies and a blazing fire, but there's nothing ersatz about the refreshments. The beers, supplied exclusively by the owners, St Peter's Brewery of Suffolk, are just what's called for, not least to wash down their knockout 'big game pie'.

*55 Britton Street, EC1M 5UQ*
*Nearest station: Farringdon*
*stpetersbrewery.co.uk/london-pub*
*@jerusalemtavern*

6

# THE LYRIC

*Showstopping beers in a characterful
Theatreland pub*

Even on a good day, it's a maelstrom around Soho,
Theatreland and Piccadilly Circus – so it's very handy
to know there's the perfect place around the corner
to pause for breath and steel yourself with a pint. But
not just any old pint – The Lyric's cup truly runneth
over in the bar department, with a compendious selection of beers, kegs and bottles. With Victorian etched
glass and panelling worthy of a stage set, plus an
upstairs restaurant with hearty pub grub, you'll soon
be begging for encores in this little West End haven.

*37 Great Windmill Street, W1D 7LT
Nearest station: Piccadilly Circus
lyricsoho.co.uk  @thelyricpub*

7

# THE QUEEN'S HEAD

*Dinky Victorian fave serving award-winning brews*

The Queen Vic in *Eastenders* isn't the only pub with a bust of Victoria; hopefully this one's never been used as a murder weapon. But you *would* be a blunt instrument not to walk five minutes from King's Cross to this sweet bow-windowed pub, full of etched glass and mirrors, where the cask ales and ciders are second to none. It appeals to academic types from nearby universities looking for a quiet pint and a Melton Mowbray pork pie, or live music around the piano on Thursdays and Sundays. Even Queen Vic would be amused.

*66 Acton Street, WC1X 9NB*
*Nearest station: King's Cross St. Pancras*
*queensheadlondon.com*
*@the_queens_head_london*

8

# THE HARP

*Paradise for real ale lovers amid tourist hell*

Hidden among the rough of substandard West End boozers, The Harp is a true diamond – a sanctuary from the Covent Garden crowds, despite its own ever-present bustle inside. It's won almost as many awards as there are gilt-framed portraits hanging on the walls. There's no better spot to nurse a proper pint (try Harvey's Sussex Best) and soak up the old-school vibe in a wingback under the ochre glow of the stained-glass windows.

*47 Chandos Place, WC2N 4HS*
*Nearest station: Charing Cross*
*harpcoventgarden.com  @theharpcoventgarden*

9

# THE CHAMPION

*Churchlike tranquillity in a splendid
Victorian setting*

Many endure the melee of Oxford Street without
ever happening upon this beautiful piece of high
Victoriana just a block away. An almost ecclesiastical
calm pervades The Champion, largely thanks to acres
of breathtaking stained glass that filters soft light
onto a hushed dark-wood interior – not to mention
Samuel Smith brewery house rules that outlaw phones,
laptops, music and swearing. The windows, depict-
ing heroes from the era, were actually added in 1989,
but you'd never guess they weren't original to this
magnificent listed building. For peace, pie and a pint,
it can hardly be beaten.

*12–13 Wells Street, W1T 3PA*
*Nearest station: Oxford Circus*

10

# SINGER TAVERN

*City glamour with an exhaustive beer list*

A dome tops an elegant 1920s building, once the London headquarters for the Singer sewing machine company, and now the home of a city pub that's anything but sew-sew (sorry). Its bright open-plan bar, tiled like a bathhouse with panelling from a 1960s executive suite, hosts an extensive range of bottled beers that's tailor-made for city highflyers. Shady *Mad Men* types will feel right at home in the moody basement cocktail bar, where rare Italian digestivi are definitely on the agenda.

*1 City Road, EC1Y 1AG*
*Nearest station: Old Street*
*singertavern.com @singertavern*

11

# THE LADY OTTOLINE

*Elegant Bloomsbury beauty with
a penchant for gin*

Meticulous interior design and an achingly tasteful
colour palette ensure that The Lady Ottoline deports
itself with the class and manner befitting its name-
sake, the literary hostess and Bloomsbury socialite,
Lady Ottoline Morrell. She's thought to be the inspi-
ration for novelist D. H. Lawrence's infamous Lady
Chatterley, whose steamy clinches with her gardener
outraged a strait-laced Britain. The pub's just as un-
buttoned: with over 50 gins to sample, there's plenty
of scope for a bit of unbridled barside passion, but
you can restore your dignity in the splendid dining
rooms upstairs.

*11A Northington Street, WC1N 2JF
Nearest station: Chancery Lane
@theladyottoline*

12

# OLD FOUNTAIN

*Gentrification-defying, family-run pub*

This free house has been in the hands of the Durrant family since 1964, and it's stayed true to its roots. From the glazed red tiles to the fish tank bizarrely propped in one corner, this is the real deal – a traditional boozer that does things its own way. The food and drink, on the other hand, is bang up-to-trend, with locally sourced produce, knockout Sunday roasts and 15 changing taps to cater to every taste. A few hours after the 5pm rush when the offices empty, it calms down enough for you to really savour its unique charms and deftly curated ales.

*3 Baldwin Street, EC1V 9NU*
*Nearest station: Old Street*
*oldfountain.co.uk  @oldfountain*

13

# THE DUKE OF RICHMOND

*Neighbourhood gastropub pressing*
*all the right buttons*

Helmed by wonder-chef Tom Oldroyd, the Duke's ever-evolving, French-tinged, seasonal menu turns the existential tension between haute cuisine and pub fayre into a harmonious marriage, spawning such glorious offspring as the crab chip butty and cap-of-ribeye burgers doused in Roquefort and béarnaise sauce. With the velvet-trimmed comforts of a pub *and* the polished quality of a respected restaurant, this is the best of both worlds with food that's out of this one.

*316 Queensbridge Road, E8 3NH*
*Nearest station: Dalston Junction*
*thedukeofrichmond.com @thedukeofrichmond*

14

# CHESHAM ARMS

*The best beer garden in east London? Probably*

Thanks to tenacious local resistance, the Chesh – as its champions call it – escaped disastrous closure in 2013. Instead, it emerged as an official 'asset of community value', and rightly so for such a dapper, real-ale stalwart. It's a special pub any time of the year, but it really comes into its own on summer evenings, when the low sun bathes the capacious beer garden with a life-enhancing glow. Get here early, as you won't be the only one wanting to soak up rays and beer in equal, voluminous quantity.

*15 Mehetabel Road, E9 6DU*
*Nearest station: Hackney Central*
*cheshamarms.com  @cheshamarms*

15

# WELL AND BUCKET

*Handsome pub revival specialising in oysters*

Some might say it's caught between the rival universes of Shoreditch and Bethnal Green, but the Well and Bucket has quality enough to create its own gravity. A refit brought out the best of the building's Victorian past after a sad few years as a leather wholesaler; feast your eyes on those glazed tiles. It really gets into its own late in the evening when the music is loud, the oysters copious, and the drinks flow freely from its centrepiece copper-topped bar. Even with the lure of Brick Lane's bagel shops across the road, you won't want to kick the Bucket.

*143 Bethnal Green Road, E2 7DG*
*Nearest station: Shoreditch High Street*
*wellandbucket.com @wellandbucket*

16

# THE COCK TAVERN

*Comfortably shabby boozer in
the heart of Hackney*

'Lots of nice beer and lovely meat', reads the board outside The Cock Tavern. How well they know us. Inside, the bare boards, Formica tables and mismatched stools create come-as-you-are homeliness without even trying. Park yourself in front of its awesome parade of pumps, featuring local brewery Howling Hops (who began their career brewing in the basement), and enjoy a pickled egg from its equally bonkers-yet-impressive selection. Garam Masala flavour, anyone?

*315 Mare Street, E8 1EJ
Nearest station: Hackney Central
thecocktavern.co.uk  @thecocktaverne8*

17

# THE PALM TREE

*Hard-nosed East End survivor still
doing it the old way*

In a park a coconut's throw from the Regent's Canal, The Palm Tree stands alone in an area devastated by the Blitz. This pristine example of a 1930s purpose-built 'improved' pub is as well preserved inside as out – and that's not even including the regulars who have been bar fixtures for decades. Rain or shine, its dim red glow, plush velvet curtains and shimmering golden wallpaper keep the harsh world beyond at bay. Come the weekend you'll be treated to live music, crooning and a proper cockney knees-up, just like old times.

*127 Grove Road, E3 5BH
Nearest station: Mile End*

18

# PROSPECT OF WHITBY

*Riverside local steeped in history*

Pitched between the Thames and Shadwell Basin, this ancient pub, dating from 1520, rises from the river at low tide on seaweed-flocked beams. Although touristy, it's the perfect spot to contemplate the smugglers, Jack tars and scoundrels who once pounded its flagstone floors and lurked in its crooked doorways – some of whom no doubt met with a hangman's noose like the one flapping eerily in the breeze beside the willow-shaded waterside garden. With history so thick and river so close, you can't do much better for salty ocean-going, buccaneering atmosphere.

*57 Wapping Wall, E1W 3SH*
*Nearest station: Wapping*
*greeneking-pubs.co.uk  @theprospectofwhitby*

Smugglers Bar

Ladies

19

# RED HAND

*Drinkers' heaven with toasties to match*

With its dark, roughly painted walls and spartan furniture, Red Hand can at first seem a little austere. But faced with a frankly gargantuan drinks list that runs the gamut from craft to gluten free to sharing bottles to natural wine on tap, you'll soon forego traditional pub comforts. There's no need to be a total ascetic, though – indulge in a top-tier sourdough toastie, oozing cheese with chorizo, sambal or some other sumptuous savoury chosen by the in-house toastie genius. It'll give you strength to stay till the small hours.

*36–38 Stoke Newington Road, N16 7XJ*
*Nearest station: Dalston Kingsland*
*red-hand.co.uk  @redhandlondon*

20

# MARKSMAN

*Trailblazing Hackney gastropub*

Award-winning chefs Tom Harris and Jon Rotheram have wowed London's critics and punters alike since they opened doors in 2015 on one of the city's finest pub dining experiences. At Marksman it's all about delicious British fare, as wholesome and nourishing as your granny's home cooking, but executed with Michelin-starred genius. But it's still a pub at heart, with all the ease, warmth and quality ale you'd expect. Just don't skip dinner, and definitely not the beef and barley buns with horseradish.

*254 Hackney Road, E2 7SJ*
*Nearest station: Hoxton*
*marksmanpublichouse.com*
*@marksman_pub*

21
# THE CLAPTON HART

*Cavernous underdressed classic pleasing all*

Less a pub, more a multi-roomed experience, The Clapton Hart truly has something for everyone: cosy drinking dens, a lively bar, an intimate dining room plus a spacious beer garden. The peeling paint job and worn wooden trim only seem to add to its threadbare charm. Whether you're after a raucous weekender, a cheeky mid-afternoon pint, the lively Thursday-night pub quiz or a quiet corner to avoid it, this place succeeds in being all things to all people, with little not to enjoy.

*231 Lower Clapton Road, E5 8EG*
*Nearest station: Clapton*
*claptonhart.com @claptonhartpub*

22

# THE PEMBURY TAVERN

*Hackney landmark given new life*
*by a local brewery*

The Pembo, as it's affectionately known, manages the rare trick of merging the yin and yang of Hackney, new-blood creatives and long-time denizens, into one giant happy whole. The Five Points Brewing Company rescued what was a terminally creaking boozer and gave it the kiss of life, without alienating the old-time regulars. They also supplied it with their full range of excellent beers, brewed literally around the corner, as well as inventive stone-baked pizza from Ace Pizzeria. They even kept the bar billiards!

*90 Amhurst Road, E8 1JH*
*Nearest station: Hackney Downs*
*pemburytavern.co.uk  @pemburytavern*

23

# THE KINGS ARMS

*Beer lovers' dream hidden off*
*Bethnal Green Road*

It may be on Buckfast Street, but this revamped corner local is all about beer – particularly the most interesting, unusual and delicious ones it can lay its hands on from around the world. Catering to the most exacting of beer enthusiasts, it also delights all-comers, being both easy on the eye as well as a perfect spot to meet and fuel up on the Shoreditch–Bethnal Green axis of fun. Don't like beer? Try the Buckfast negroni (made with the infamous tonic wine), the perfect turbocharged aperitif.

*11A Buckfast Street, E2 6EY*
*Nearest station: Bethnal Green*
*thekingsarmspub.com  @kingsarmspub*

24

# JOYCE

*Friendly faces in a former undertakers*

A white-tiled bar in a former funeral parlour risks recreating the sterile chill of a morgue – but not at Joyce, a local that offers Brockley's warmest welcome. The staff can't wait to bend your ear about the latest local micro-distillery on tap (which also pour wine and cocktails), or to host their favourite producers for 'meet the maker' events – far merrier than the 'meet thy maker' events of the previous occupants. Despite the stern interior, it's as intimately comfortable as your front room, and conversation is as free-flowing as its top-end libations.

*294 Brockley Road, SE4 2RA*
*Nearest station: Brockley*
*joycebrockley.com  @joyce.brockley*

25

# THE KINGS ARMS

*Old-time local on a picturesque Dickensian street*

There's a simple beauty to the Georgian terraces of Roupell Street that make it feel a million miles from the crowds of Waterloo station and the South Bank nearby. Sitting at the heart of this architectural treasure is The Kings Arms. Still keeping a separation between its public and saloon bars, it's as old-school as they come, but all enlivened by an ever-changing supply of real ales. Thai food is served in the back area, which the pub describes as 'farmhouse', but it's no less charming than any other part of this wonderful boozer.

*25 Roupell Street, SE1 8TB*
*Nearest station: Waterloo*
*thekingsarmslondon.co.uk  @thekingsarmsldn*

26

# THE GARRISON

*Foodie stronghold in Bermondsey's
creative quarter*

The Garrison makes the bold claim to be the home of 'London's best roasts'. Without getting into the semantics of 'best', let's just say that this pub's so popular you'll need to book Sunday lunch well in advance to decide for yourself. It's no one-trick pony either, offering seasonal menus and stunningly good breakfasts, lunches and dinners every day of the week in its whimsical dining room, complete with mismatched furniture and vintage lampshades. Need time to digest that extra Yorkshire pud? Try Sunday film night in the underground cinema room.

*99–101 Bermondsey Street, SE1 3XB*
*Nearest station: London Bridge*
*thegarrison.co.uk  @thegarrisonse1*

27

# THE MAYFLOWER

*Maritime masterpiece overlooking the Thames*

For such a historic pub, it's surprising it was only 1957 when it became The Mayflower – after the famous ship, once moored nearby, that carried the Pilgrim Fathers to America. But everything else is properly old: a 16th-century pub in an 18th-century building on a cobbled backstreet, fitted with a creaking dark-wood interior worthy of a spume-sprayed quarterdeck. It doesn't get much more nautical than this, especially if you're out on the riverside jetty-cum-garden; at high tide the water's so close it's practically splashing your pint.

*117 Rotherhithe Street, SE16 4NF*
*Nearest station: Rotherhithe*
*mayflowerpub.co.uk  @mayflowerpub*

28

# THE WHITE HORSE

*Great London beers and kebabs*

With its clipped trees, trellises, hanging baskets and house plants, the less observant among us might mistake The White Horse for a garden centre. But a pub it is through and through, and has been since the 1800s. A voluminous interior, including a gaming area for darts and pool deftly separated from the bar by a standalone screen, lends itself to full-on revelry at the weekends courtesy of live music and top DJs. The kitchen's open every day, serving either Sunday lunches or Babber's mind-blowing chargrilled kebabs.

*20–22 Peckham Rye, SE15 4JR*
*Nearest station: Peckham Rye*
*whitehorsepeckham.co.uk @whitehorsepeckham*
*babberkebab.co.uk @babber_peckham*

29
# THE ANCHOR & HOPE

*A paragon of the gastropub*

If only more so-called gastropubs were like this: a menu that changes day to day depending on what's in the kitchen; surprising new dishes (spiced duck hearts on sesame flatbread); plenty of crowd-pleasers like three-cheese hazelnut soufflé followed by hot chocolate pot with stem ginger ice cream; wines for everything; and, most of all, the feel and décor of a proper pub – informal, unfussy, no-reservations busy, hard-scrubbed tables and weathered boards. Truly delicious.

*36 The Cut, SE1 8LP*
*Nearest station: Southwark*
*anchorandhopepub.co.uk  @anchorhopecut*

30
# PRINCE OF PECKHAM

*Community hub of a pub with a Caribbean flavour*

Peckham has come a long way since the era of Del Boy and Rodders – it's now one of London's coolest neighbourhoods, and Prince of Peckham is king of the castle. Owner Clement Ogbonnaya wants everyone and anyone (spot the huge 'Welcome to Peckham' mural outside?) to rock up, chill, dance, party and bottomless brunch. Among many local options, try Brixton Atlantic pale ale to quench the spice of the buttermilk-dipped jerk chicken and southern-fried cauli buns cooked up by their drolly named kitchen suppliers, White Men Can't Jerk. Or just hit the Wray & Nephew overproof rum. Lovely jubbly.

*1 Clayton Road, SE15 5JA*
*Nearest station: Queens Road Peckham*
*princeofpeckham.co.uk  @princepeckham*
*whitemencantjerk.com  @whitemencantjerk*

31

# THE IVY HOUSE

*London's first cooperatively owned pub*

Bunting, face paints and brass bands abound at The Ivy's summer fetes, where you'll end up dancing in the street – hang on to that pint! In colder months, sprawling across a chesterfield by the fireside is just as enjoyable. And throughout the year, at the back of this listed building, raucous evenings of live music, leaning towards folk and indie, play out on a real theatre stage draped in red and gold. There are even live-band karaoke nights, where you might just find yourself unleashing your inner Elvis.

*40 Stuart Road, SE15 3BE*
*Nearest station: Nunhead*
*ivyhousenunhead.com  @ivyhousenunhead*

32
# MC & SONS

*Family-run Irish pub serving the*
*Emerald Isle's greatest brews*

Mc & Sons have channelled the spirit of Dublin's Temple Bar into a quiet corner of Southwark – and made that rare thing, an Irish pub that really *is* an Irish pub (plus Thai kitchen!). The McElhinney family from County Kildare are proud to serve fine Irish beers, including Franciscan Well from Cork, and regularly host live Irish music. Crucially, the Guinness goes down well here – perhaps it's the Hibernian charm that makes it so quaffable. Get the ten-person snug with its own private bar hatch, or just grab a seat, a pint, and a bag of Taytos and settle in for the night. Sláinte!

*160 Union Street, SE1 0LH*
*Nearest station: Southwark*
*mcandsonslondon.com @mcandsonslondon*

33

# THE KING & CO

*Free-spirited retreat with plenty to taste and do*

As an independent free house, The King & Co does as it jolly well pleases. It handpicks an eclectic range of craft beers and wines, puts on quiz nights, live music and lively special events, and even gives street-food pop-ups the run of the kitchen. The same creative liberty applies to the décor, which includes a 70s three-piece so hideous that everyone wants a go. In this charmingly quirky venue, you can relax and be surprised all at once.

*100 Clapham Park Road, SW4 7BZ*
*Nearest station: Clapham Common*
*thekingandco.uk  @thekingandco*

34

# THE UNION TAVERN

*Dreamy canalside retreat for whiling time away*

For a little slice of Venice with the added benefit of London's finest craft and cask beers, you can't do much better than the slender garden of The Union Tavern, running directly alongside the Grand Union Canal. There's plenty of space for lounging within the airy interior while you attend to the likes of some crispy squid or beef brisket. In the summer, step outside and enjoy a cold one (or two) in the shade of its large awning, while the sunshine lingers late into the evening and narrowboats drift idly by.

*45 Woodfield Road, W9 2BA*
*Nearest station: Westbourne Park*
*union-tavern.co.uk  @uniontavern*

35

# THE QUEEN'S ARMS

*The antidote to the crowds of South Kensington*

Stumbling upon The Queen's Arms after a day traips-
ing around exhibitions in South Ken is guaranteed
to put the spring back in your step. It's a true retreat,
in elegant powder-blue on a quiet cobbled mews,
where a beautiful set of curved double doors opens
to reveal a classic horseshoe bar. A stylish dining
room beyond dishes up well-executed pub paradigms
like pie and mash, fish and chips and succulent burgers, plus excellent cask and craft ales. Relax, refresh
and recover.

*30 Queen's Gate Mews, SW7 5QL*
*Nearest station: Gloucester Road*
*thequeensarmskensington.co.uk*
*@thequeensarmskensington*

36

# THE MALL TAVERN

*Relaxed Notting Hill hangout for pure indulgence*

The cheeseburgers at The Mall Tavern are to die for:
perfectly seasoned beef zealously doused in tangy
sauce and melted cheese, leaving slicks of translucent
fat trailing down your wrists. Low candlelight and
the hum of an evening crowd provides ideal camou-
flage for your exploration of the menu (which has
plenty besides burgers, such as crispy seabass and 23
beer taps), while the glimmer of chandeliers adds a
dash of west London glamour. But it's actually as
laid-back as you like, with any air of pretension left
at the doorstep.

*71 Palace Gardens Terrace, W8 4RU*
*Nearest station: Notting Hill Gate*
*themallw8.com  @malltavern*

TOWN · HILLS → 4.6%, £5.10
4 KERNEL · WALTI PALE → 4.8%, £5.60
5 SIREN · HAZY PALE → 5.6%, £5.00
6 LUCKY SAINT · LAGER → 4.0%, £5.40 ⅔
7 UMBRELLA CIDER → 0.5%, £6.20
8 BEAVERTOWN · NECK OIL → 5%, £5.30
9 PROJECT 88 · LAGER → 4%, £4.3%, £6.00
10 PROJECT 88 · PALE ALE → 4%, £5.30
11 KERNEL · CENTENNIAL → 4%, £6.00
12 HACKEY · UNICORN DON XPA → 6.9%, £5.40 ⅔
13 ONE MILE END · BAVARIAN WHEAT → 4%, £4.50
14 ONE MILE END · JUICY → 5%, £4.4%, £4 ⅔
15 UMBRELLA · RHUBARB CIDER → 4.9%, £4 ⅔
16 HOPKINS · CBD PALE ALE → 5%, £6.00
17 GUINNESS · STOUT → 4.2%, £6.20
18 KERNEL · EXPORT PORTER → 6.3%, £5.40
19 HAMMERTON · PEANUT CRUNCH → 5.5%, £5.00 ⅔
20 HACKEY · BOOGIE VAN IPA → 5.5%, £4.50 ⅔
21 HAMMERTON · RED BERRY SOUR → 4.6%, £5

**and 3 cask handles**

37

# THE WINDSOR CASTLE

*Charming Georgian number with*
*princely interiors*

It's less a castle, more a village local secreted away
in the backstreets behind Kensington's tourist hot-
spots. But when it was built in the 1820s, you could
apparently see the real Windsor Castle shimmering
in the distance. A doorway heavily laden with Virginia
creeper leads to a string of stately oak-panelled drinking rooms, worthy of the pub's regal name. And to
the rear is the crown jewel: a suntrap of a beer garden
surrounded by a quadrangle of whitewashed walls
that defend your peace and quiet from the city beyond.

*114 Campden Hill Road, w8 7ar*
*Nearest station: Notting Hill Gate*
*thewindsorcastlekensington.co.uk*
*@windsorcastlew8*

38

# THE WHITE HORSE

*Legendary alehouse overlooking Parsons Green*

A favourite of the late Michael Jackson (no, not that one – the much-revered and missed beer author), The White Horse continues to maintain its reputation for serving some of the finest real ale in the capital. A lush refurb worthy of the pub's nickname 'the Sloaney Pony' effaced some of its timeworn charm, but the revelous atmosphere, particularly during its beer festivals, remains. Get a Pilsner Urquell straight from a copper tank (the UK's first pub to offer this), fill up on a bottomless brunch, or simply sink into one of the velvet wingbacks.

*1–3 Parsons Green, SW6 4UL*
*Nearest station: Parsons Green*
*whitehorsesw6.com @whitehorsesw6*

39

# THE HARWOOD ARMS

*The best of British at London's first and only
Michelin-starred pub*

With so many awards and plaudits, The Harwood
Arms sets lofty expectations. Even though its game-
leaning, updated British cuisine is widely regarded
as the best in the business, there's no reason to feel
intimidated. This is still a pub through and through,
with regulars swilling cask ales at the bar and nib-
bling on signature Scotch eggs. But most come for
the dining, and particularly the sensational nose-to-
tail menu (venison tartare or perhaps crispy pig's
head, anyone?), now enhanced with delicious meat-
free options, plus veg from the rooftop garden. Yum.

*Walham Grove, SW6 1QP*
*Nearest station: Fulham Broadway*
*harwoodarms.com @harwoodarms*

40

# THE FLASK

*Village-inn vibes in the heart of Highgate*

After the steep haul uphill to Highgate Village, there is no better spot to slake your thirst than The Flask. Nourished by the rarefied air above the city smog and opposite the capital's highest church, its leafy garden evokes the peace and prosperity of a home-counties inn. When in the full bloom of early summer, this historic pub's Georgian frontage is spectacular. Come winter, the cosy interior and vaulted snugs are just as enticing, and its Sunday roasts are always piled high.

*77 Highgate West Hill, N6 6BU*
*Nearest station: Highgate*
*theflaskhighgate.com @the.flask.n6*

41

# THE WENLOCK ARMS

*Quiet hideaway that comes to life for Friday jazz*

Hidden behind a dogleg of canal in the no man's land between Angel and Old Street, the Wenlock *really* has to be searched out. It's a wonder how it ever gets busy, but after a visit to this deeply comforting old-school boozer and a sip of some of the best cask ale in London, you'll understand. You'll fall in love with its quirks, like the toasted sandwich maker behind the bar that dominates the minimal menu, and the trio who appear like clockwork on Fridays at 9pm to fill the room with jazz classics.

*26 Wenlock Road, N1 7TA*
*Nearest station: Old Street*
*wenlockarms.com @wenlockarms*

42

# THE AXE

*Revamped beer haven and Stokey favourite*

There's no signage outside The Axe. Clearly the owners are confident they can do away with such niceties, believing they have a destination venue on their hands. They're right; The Axe hits the target with a resounding *thwack,* and has quickly built up a strong local following. Book yourself in for a lazy Sunday lunch, fully upgradable with outstanding cauliflower cheese, and devote the afternoon to deep-dive research of its mind-meltingly vast and exotic beer list.

*18 Northwold Road, N16 7HR*
*Nearest station: Stoke Newington*
*theaxepub.com  @theaxepub*

PINT
MAKEMAKE
FLANDERS RED ALE
6%
PINT
BROUWERIJ RODENBACH
GRAND CRU
8%
£4.00
PINT
BRASSERIE DUPONT
CERVESIA
ANCIENT HERBED ALE
5.5%
£4.00
PINT
NEVEL ARTISAN ALES
ALM
WILD ALE
PINT
LONDON BEER FACTORY
LA PASSION
TART SAISON
6.5%
£4.20
PINT
VERDANT
UNFURLING OF THE HOOKS
DIPA
8%
£4.20
PINT
OMNIPOLLO/ SIREN
LORELEI '2019'
IMP. PORTER
10.5%
£5.00

43

# THE HOLLY BUSH

*History and tranquillity above Hampstead Village*

Hidden in plain sight among petite terraced Georgian houses in one of Hampstead's postcard-perfect hilltop backstreets, The Holly Bush is a world removed from the scramble of the city. Wood panelling, floorboards and seasoned leather complete the sense of timelessness, while upstairs, the Romney Room showcases the pub's historic splendour. It's worth booking for special occasions – not that you should need one to pay this comely pub a visit.

*22 Hollymount, NW3 6SG*
*Nearest station: Hampstead*
*hollybushhampstead.co.uk*
*@thehollybushpubhampstead*

44

# SMOKEHOUSE

*High-end dining and a huge choice of real ales*

Natural light, clean white walls, bare boards, old wooden furniture, and a menu scrawled on a black-board above an open kitchen are all familiar features of the photogenic gastropub. But there's an integrity to Smokehouse lacking in most: a commitment to the best small independent suppliers, breweries and wineries that ensures you'll be well catered for, not least at its 20 taps of fine craft beer. Add a talent for the charcoal barbeque and oak-smoked meats, and you're guaranteed intense, lip-smacking flavours, too.

*63–69 Canonbury Road, N1 2DG*
*Nearest station: Essex Road*
*smokehouseislington.co.uk  @smokehousen1*

45

# THE THREE JOHNS

*NYC cool for good times and fine beer*

Before The Three Johns opened, the clientele of this venue were typically clad in black leather and liberally applied eyeshadow. Things have changed since its goth days. High panelled ceilings and exposed brickwork now recall the easy sophistication of a Williamsburg beer joint, while the sourdough pizza would happily hold its own on the Lower East Side; especially when scarfed down with a Stone & Wood Pacific Ale, to name just one of many craft options. Stay for a bourbon and, at the weekend, dance like no one is watching into the small hours.

*73 White Lion Street, N1 9PF*
*Nearest station: Angel*
*three-johns.com @thethreejohns*

46
# THE JOLLY BUTCHERS
*Brilliant Indian cooking and top-quality ales*

Pillars, ornate arches and a glossy cherry-and-grey paint job lend the air of a railway tavern to this pleasantly ramshackle venue. But there's nothing slapdash about the cooking, thanks to Booma's kitchen residency and some of North London's best Indian food. Think perfectly charred chunks of spiced paneer, Chettinaad pork ribs stacked high, indulgently creamy dal makhani and duck kathi rolls that burn in the best possible way. Thankfully, there's also an extensive and well-researched multinational beer and real ale menu to temper all that spice.

*204 Stoke Newington High Street, N16 7HU*
*Nearest station: Stoke Newington*
*jollybutchers.co.uk  @thejollybutchers*

47

# THE HIGH CROSS

*Pint-size local in an old public lav*

Given the compact size of this former public convenience, you'll wonder which laws of quantum physics The High Cross had to break to squeeze in ten beer taps and a kitchen – let alone the whale-sized portions of fish and chips (a must order) that emerge from within. With 1920s mock Tudor on the outside and original white tiles inside, it's a building still giving sweet relief to Tottenham locals (and Spurs fans on match days), while the close quarters encourage cross-table banter and bonhomie. Come to spend a penny, spend the night.

*350 High Road, N17 9HT*
*Nearest station: Bruce Grove*
*@highcrosslondon*

48

# THE DRAPERS ARMS

*Fine dining in handsome surroundings*

Not many pubs can boast tympana, Doric pilasters *and* plain-eared architraves – but then few have the architectural grandeur of The Drapers. A listed building in eggshell blue, its tall windows and light spaces trigger just the right mindful clarity for perusing a tantalising seasonal menu. Whether it's a quick pit-stop to gulp down a couple of rock oysters in the beer garden, a leisurely Sunday roast, or a long evening of unbridled gluttony in the dining room, a visit to The Drapers will always be sure to reward heart, belly and soul.

*44 Barnsbury Street, N1 1ER*
*Nearest stations: Essex Road*
*thedrapersarms.com @thedrapersarms*

49

# THE PINEAPPLE

*Cherished backstreet gem and*
*quintessential local*

Dating from 1868, a time when the pineapple re-presented all anyone could want from a fruit, The Pineapple is still all you could want from a pub. Unsurprisingly, locals are bananas for it, and successfully fought to save its striking duck-egg blue frontage, complete with bas-relief pineapples, and gorgeous (now listed) mirrored bar from the developers' sledgehammers. Down by a quiet Victorian mews in Kentish Town, it's well worth the detour for the superbly kept real ale, regular special events and authentic good cheer.

*51 Leverton Street, NW5 2NX*
*Nearest station: Kentish Town*
*thepineapplepubnw5.com @thepineapplepub*

50

# THE BULL & LAST

*Foodie favourite on the edge of Hampstead Heath*

After a lengthy stomp across the Heath, the sight of The Bull & Last is welcome indeed. You'll know from the smell of cooking that this will be way more than a pit stop for tired legs. Prepare to lose yourself in food reveries about Merrie England: Brixham crab, Hereford prime rib, North Essex shorthorn beef, all done with grace and skill far surpassing pub norms. Swap thoughts of the walk back for a scoop of Ferrero Rocher ice cream and another pint, as the setting sun creeps low through tall windows.

*168 Highgate Road, NW5 1QS*
*Nearest station: Gospel Oak*
*thebullandlast.co.uk  @thebullandlast*

51

# THE SOUTHAMPTON ARMS

*Stripped-back boozer dedicated
to simple pleasures*

Tuesday night is jazz night at The Southampton Arms – but don't let that put you off. In fact, this is the best time to visit for the toe-tapping music that'll have you cheering for more. There's no faffing about here, no phone, no reservations, no credit cards, and for that matter, not a lot of space – just steely-eyed focus on its eclectic range of independent beers and ciders, and 'lovely meat' – manifesting as juicy pork baps and award-winning pork pies. It works; you can't beat simple things done well.

*139 Highgate Road, NW5 1LE
Nearest station: Gospel Oak
thesouthamptonarms.co.uk  @southamptonnw5*

# ABOUT
# HOXTON MINI PRESS

Hoxton Mini Press is a small indie publisher based in east London. We make books about London – we love and breathe this city – and always with a dedication to good photography and lovely production. When we started the company people told us 'print was dead'. That inspired us. Books are no longer about information but objects in their own right: things to collect and own and inspire. Cheers to that.

*www.hoxtonminipress.com*

# INDEX

# CONTRIBUTORS

*Matthew Curtis* is an award-winning freelance beer writer and co-founder of the online food and drink magazine *Pellicle*. He'd never have guessed he'd be writing part of this guide while pubs were in lockdown and is now desperate for a pint he hasn't poured himself.

*Harry Adès* grew up in London next door to – and now lives exactly 36 paces away from – a very fine pub. Despite that, he has written many books, including another in this series: *An Opinionated Guide to London Green Spaces*.

Photographer *Orlando Gili* is a born-and-bred Londoner; shooting this book found him revisiting memories of first dates, nights out and even a former weekend job pulling pints at The French House. His most recent photo book, *Trivial Pursuits,* is also published by Hoxton Mini Press.